Teens and Suicide

Cherese Cartlidge

San Diego, CA

© 2017 ReferencePoint Press, Inc.
Printed in the United States

For more information, contact:
ReferencePoint Press, Inc.
PO Box 27779
San Diego, CA 92198
www.ReferencePointPress.com

LIBRARY OF CONGRESS CATALOGING-IN-PUBLICATION DATA

Name: Cartlidge, Cherese, author.
Title: Teens and suicide / Cherese Cartlidge.
Description: San Diego, CA : ReferencePoint Press, [2017] | Series: Teen
   mental health | Audience: Grade 9 to 12. | Includes bibliographical
   references and index.
Identifiers: LCCN 2016040557 (print) | LCCN 2016052384 (ebook) | ISBN
   9781682821312 (hardback) | ISBN 9781682821336 (eBook)
Subjects: LCSH: Teenagers--Suicidal behavior--Juvenile literature. |
   Suicide--Juvenile literature. | Depression in adolescence--Juvenile
   literature.
Classification: LCC HV6546 .C38 2017 (print) | LCC HV6546 (ebook) | DDC
   362.280835--dc23
LC record available at https://lccn.loc.gov/2016040557

CONTENTS

A Vulnerable Population

High school sophomore David Molak of San Antonio, Texas, was a fun-loving kid and Eagle Scout. He played on his school's basketball team and was a fan of the San Antonio Spurs. He also enjoyed playing Monopoly with his parents and two older brothers—and he usually won. He often worked out at the local gym and was even named the gym's Athlete of the Month during his sophomore year. And at sixteen, he was already planning to follow in his older brothers' footsteps by attending Texas A&M University.

But Molak's life began to deteriorate when fellow students started to bully him through social media. The cyberbullies were attacking him over his physical appearance and berating him for his relationship with a popular girl at school. In an effort to help stop the bullying, his parents transferred him to a private Christian school. But even switching schools did not help; the cruel Instagram posts, group texts, and videos continued over the course of several months, and he began to sink into a dark depression. "He lost faith in people,"[1] says his older brother, Cliff Molak. "These people were bashing him for no reason. He did not do anything to them besides having an attractive girlfriend. He was just a pure-spirited guy. But, they crushed his spirit and took away his motivation to do anything."[2]

One night David received a series of bullying text messages that devastated him. Cliff describes David's reaction to the texts: "He stared off into the distance for what seemed like an hour. I could feel his pain. It was a tangible pain."[3] During the night David made the heartbreaking decision to end his life. On the morning of January 4, 2016, he was found dead; he had hung himself in his own backyard.

Teens Vulnerable to Suicide

The news media is full of stories about teens who have taken their own lives to end the torment of bullying. And although bullying—especially cyberbullying—is a common factor in many teen suicides, it is far from the only one. There are many other things that can lead teens into depression and drive them to kill themselves.

Adolescence can be a difficult time of life, but it is especially so for teens who suffer from depression. Because teens are young and inexperienced, many lack the skills needed to cope with depression—especially when depressive thoughts turn to suicide. Psychologist Lucie Hemmen says the stress of adolescence makes teens vulnerable to depression and suicidal thinking. "Emotional turmoil is definitely part of being a teen. With brains undergoing huge changes, hormones surging, fragile self-confidence and scant life experience to counterbalance daily stressors, it's no wonder they're vulnerable."[4]

Some teens are more vulnerable to depression and suicidal thoughts than others. This is because some kids may not be well equipped to deal with the challenges they face as they grow up. "Many teens who attempt or die by suicide have a mental health condition," the Mayo Clinic explains. "As a result, they have trouble coping with the stress of being a teen, such as dealing with rejection, failure, breakups and family turmoil. They might also be unable to see

> "Emotional turmoil is definitely part of being a teen. With brains undergoing huge changes, hormones surging, fragile self-confidence and scant life experience to counterbalance daily stressors, it's no wonder they're vulnerable."[4]
>
> —Lucie Hemmen, a psychologist in Santa Cruz, California

Adolescence can be a difficult time of life, especially for those who suffer from depression. Many teens lack the life experiences and skills to cope with depression; without help, they sometimes turn to suicide.

that they can turn their lives around—and that suicide is a permanent response, not a solution, to a temporary problem."[5]

A Devastating Issue

The loss of a human life due to suicide is a devastating occurrence, and it is especially wrenching when a young person takes his or her own life. Each year thousands of adolescents commit suicide, usually as the result of deep inner turmoil. In the aftermath of their untimely deaths, friends and loved ones are left struggling to understand their heartrending decision. "For a teenager to be so unbearably unhappy that he would choose to kill himself is something that is almost too painful for a parent to think about,"[6] says Mark Gregston, founder and director of Heartlight, a residential counseling center for struggling teens in Longview, Texas.

Depression and suicidal thinking constitute a serious issue among young people that too often ends in tragedy. Those who do not receive treatment or who lack a support group can spiral out of control until they feel that suicide is the only answer. Sometimes even those who do get help and have supportive family and friends kill themselves. Treatment and support can prevent some suicides but not all.

> "For a teenager to be so unbearably unhappy that he would choose to kill himself is something that is almost too painful for a parent to think about."[6]
>
> —Mark Gregston, founder and director of the Heartlight residential counseling center in Longview, Texas

CHAPTER ONE

The Problem of Teen Suicide

Suicide is a significant problem in the United States. Each year roughly half a million people of all ages are admitted to hospital emergency rooms with self-inflicted injuries, according to the Centers for Disease Control and Prevention (CDC). In 2014 more than forty-two thousand people killed themselves in the United States. The issue of suicide is not confined to adults—suicide is a serious problem for teens, too. In April 2016, for instance, seventeen-year-old Brendan Manley, a Madisonville, Louisiana, high school senior and member of the school's swim team, drove his mother's car to a secluded area and shot himself. He was a good student who was planning to enter Loyola University in the fall. He had a close relationship with his parents and two older brothers, and he gave no signs to his family or his swim coach that he was contemplating suicide.

Sadly, Manley was just one of thousands of teens who killed themselves that year. In fact, thousands of teenagers commit suicide every year in the United States. According to the American Academy of Child & Adolescent Psychiatry (AACAP), teens who are struggling with overwhelming pressures in their lives may turn to suicide. The AACAP states:

> Teenagers experience strong feelings of stress, confusion, self-doubt, pressure to succeed, financial uncertainty, and other fears while growing up. For some teenagers, divorce, the formation of a new family with step-parents and step-siblings, or moving to a new community can be very unsettling and can intensify self-doubts. For some teens, suicide may appear to be a solution to their problems and stress.[7]

Teen suicide takes place every day, in every state in the United States. The means used by teens to end their own lives may vary from one individual to the next, and the rate of teen suicide may vary by demographics such as geographic location, sex, race, and ethnicity. But no matter the circumstances, suicide is a devastating tragedy—especially when a young person makes the choice to end his or her own life.

How Common Is Teen Suicide?

Many people think the problem of teen suicide exists only among older teens, rather than younger teens and tweens. Yet even very young kids have killed themselves, such as Colin Fraley, a ten-year-old Ohio boy who fatally shot himself in 2016. In fact, each year in the United States, an average of 4,600 youths aged 10 to 24 take their lives. In 2014, the most recent year for which figures are available, 425 kids aged 10 to 14 and 5,079 youths aged 15 to 24 committed suicide, according to the CDC. But the true number of teen deaths due to suicide may actually be even higher than the official numbers reflect, because some may have been reported as accidental deaths.

The Society for the Prevention of Teen Suicide reports that every two hours and eleven minutes, one person under age twenty-five commits suicide in the United States. Despite this frequency, teens have a much lower suicide rate than adults in the United States. In 2014, according to the American Foundation for Suicide Prevention, youths aged fifteen to twenty-four had a suicide rate of 11.6 per 100,000, compared to the rate of 19.2 for adults aged forty-five to sixty-five. Figures from the CDC also show that teens commit suicide at a lower rate than adults; of the 42,773 total suicides

> "Teenagers experience strong feelings of stress, confusion, self-doubt, pressure to succeed, financial uncertainty, and other fears while growing up. . . . For some teens, suicide may appear to be a solution to their problems and stress."[7]
>
> —The American Academy of Child & Adolescent Psychiatry

in 2014, youths aged twenty-four and younger accounted for 5,504.

Youth Contemplating Suicide

As sobering as these numbers are, experts believe that many more people attempt suicide than complete it. "We know that completed suicides are but the tip of the iceberg,"[8] says Sally C. Curtin, a statistician who led a study on youth suicides for the National Center for Health Statistics (NCHS), which is part of the CDC.

Although no complete count is kept of suicide attempts in the United States, each year the CDC collects information from hospitals on nonfatal injuries from self-harm. The CDC estimates that among the general population, there are about twenty-five attempted suicides for every completed suicide in the United States each year. That number is even higher for adolescents—as many as fifty to one hundred attempts for every successful suicide, according to Benjamin Shain, a child psychiatrist in Illinois. He points out that it can sometimes be difficult to determine whether a young person's actions qualify as a suicide attempt. "If they take 50 pills, that's an overt attempt," Shain says. However, he adds, "if they take eight pills thinking I might die that's an attempt in my book too."[9]

The Youth Suicide Prevention Program, a nonprofit organization that works to reduce teen suicide, says that teens who have attempted suicide once are at high risk of trying again. "A youth who has attempted to end his/her life has a higher risk of later dying by suicide; research has shown that between 5 and 11 percent of people who survive a suicide attempt go on to die from suicide,"[10] the organization states.

When teens attempt to take their own lives—whether those attempts are successful or not—it is a heartbreaking event. But there are even more kids who are seriously depressed and have suicidal thoughts without actually making an attempt. The exact number of kids who contemplate suicide is difficult to determine, in part because there is no specific test that can identify every potentially suicidal person. But according to the AACAP, 10 per-

Suicide Is Second Leading Cause of Death Among Youth

The prevalence of suicide as a cause of death among teens and young adults is a serious concern. According to the CDC, in 2014 (the latest year for which data are available), 5,504 individuals aged ten to twenty-four killed themselves in the United States. Of that group, the largest number of suicides involved teens and young adults. Only accidents, such as car crashes and unintentional drug overdoses, took more lives among ten- to twenty-four-year-olds than suicide.

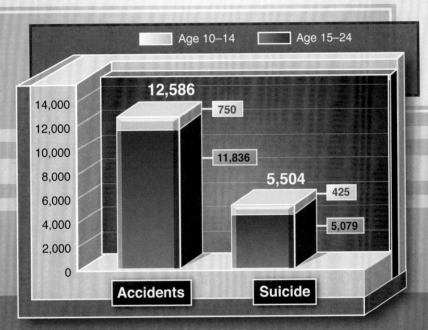

Source: Centers for Disease Control and Prevention, "10 Leading Causes of Death by Age Group, United States—2014," 2014.www.cdc.gov.

cent of all teens think about suicide at one point or another. And a 2015 CDC survey of US students in ninth through twelfth grades found that while 8.6 percent reported they had attempted suicide in the twelve months prior to the survey, 14.6 percent said they had made a suicide plan, and 17.7 percent said they had seriously considered suicide. The fact that only 2.8 percent of the students in the CDC survey had made an attempt that resulted in an injury or required medical attention helps illustrate the difficulty involved in ascertaining the true number of kids who are suffering from suicidal thoughts. "These numbers underestimate

Dispelling Myths

There are many common myths surrounding suicide. One of the most common—and potentially most harmful—misperceptions is that talking about suicide can lead a person to attempt suicide. The reality, however, is that allowing a person who is depressed or suicidal to express his or her feelings openly can be extremely helpful. And talking about suicide with a person actually reduces the risk he or she will make a suicide attempt, according to the Jason Foundation, an organization that works to prevent teen suicide.

Another myth is that a person who threatens suicide is not really serious about actually killing him- or herself. "Suicide is not a normal response to stress," says the National Institute of Mental Health. "It is however, a sign of extreme distress, not a harmless bid for attention." Indeed, a suicide threat or attempt represents a call for help in dealing with pain and depression. Therefore, any threat or attempt must be taken seriously.

A third common myth is that depression and suicidal thinking are rare in adolescents. But the truth is that both are common in teens as well as adults and even exist in children. In fact, the CDC reports that suicide is one of the leading causes of death for youths aged ten and up.

National Institute of Mental Health, "Suicide Prevention," 2015. www.nimh.nih.gov.

this problem," says the CDC. "Many people who have suicidal thoughts or make suicide attempts never seek services."[11]

The Teen Suicide Rate Is Climbing

Although other causes of death in the United States are on the decline, in April 2016 the NCHS released a report that indicates the suicide rate is climbing for every age group under age seventy-five in the United States. The report states that the suicide rate for all ages, including teens, climbed steadily from 1999 to 2014. And the report shows the suicide rate for teens is increasing for both males and females. "I've been losing sleep over this, quite honestly," says Curtin. "You can't just say it's confined to one age group or another for males and females. Truly at all ages people are at risk for this, and our youngest have some of the highest percent increases."[12]

According to the 2016 NCHS report, from 1999 to 2014 the suicide rate among teen girls saw a much sharper increase than the rate among teen boys. For males aged 10 to 14, the rate increased 37 percent during this fifteen-year time frame, and the rate for males aged 15 to 24 increased 8 percent during the same time frame. During the same time period, the rate for females aged 15 to 24 increased 50 percent, and for females aged 10 to 14, the rate increased 200 percent—the largest percent increase by far of any age group or sex.

Experts have several theories about why the suicide rate for young girls tripled over the course of fifteen years. Arielle Sheftall, who works at the Center for Suicide Prevention and Research at the Research Institute at Nationwide Children's Hospital in Columbus, Ohio, suggests that the earlier onset of puberty may be to blame. Girls tend to hit puberty at around age eleven, although studies have found that girls today tend to start their periods earlier than in the past. Sheftall believes this could be contributing to the huge jump in the number of suicides among girls in this age group. "It's usually been referred to as the storm-and-stress period of life because there's just a lot of change happening all at one time," says Sheftall. "Research has shown that puberty, unfortunately, is associated with the onset of psychological disorders, specifically depression."[13] Although this theory has not been studied extensively, Sheftall and her colleagues maintain it is one possible explanation.

Psychologist Steve Hinshaw has a different theory for the jump in the suicide rate among teen girls in recent years. He suggests the increase has to do with the fact that the Internet has made their every emotional struggle public knowledge. Thanks to the proliferation of cell phones, texting, and social media, girls today are often not able to work through these struggles in private. "Let's say things aren't going well in middle or high school and you email someone about it," Hinshaw says. "Soon it's all over everyone else's email, text messages, MySpace, Facebook. Everyone knows what's going on in your life and they're all talking about it. You can't escape it."[14]

Rather than working through their emotional struggles in private, today's teens (especially girls) often reveal their innermost thoughts through texts and social media. One expert says this might help explain the jump in the suicide rate for teen girls.

Despite all the theories, experts do not know for certain what is behind the huge increase in the suicide rate among teen girls. "We don't know what's going on, to be quite honest," says Sheftall. "We have thoughts, that maybe it's this, maybe it's that. It's really hard to pinpoint one specific risk factor that really, truly is driving this trend. . . . It's frustrating because you want to never ever see these trends increase."[15]

A Leading Cause of Death

Not only is the suicide rate among adolescents and young adults increasing, it is among the leading causes of death for this age group. According to the Jason Foundation, an organization that works to prevent teen suicide, "More teenagers and young adults die from suicide than from cancer, heart disease, AIDS, birth defects, stroke, pneumonia, influenza, and chronic lung disease, COMBINED."[16] Indeed, today suicide ranks among the top three causes of death for teens and young adults in the United States. The other two leading causes are homicide and accidents, which include unintentional injuries such as car crashes and inadvertent poisonings.

For youth of all ages, accidents are the leading cause of death. According to the CDC, in 2014 suicide was the second-leading cause of death for young people aged ten to twenty-four in the United States, after accidents. In fact, by 2014 suicide had replaced homicide as the second-leading cause of death for those aged fifteen to twenty-four. The prevalence of suicide as a cause of teen death is deeply concerning to health officials and others. "Suicide and suicide attempts are serous public health problems that devastate individuals, families and communities,"[17] notes Ileana Arias, former director of the CDC's National Center for Injury Prevention and Control.

> "More teenagers and young adults die from suicide than from cancer, heart disease, AIDS, birth defects, stroke, pneumonia, influenza, and chronic lung disease, COMBINED."[16]
>
> —The Jason Foundation, an organization that works to prevent teen suicide

Who Is at Highest Risk?

Suicide prevalence in the United States varies by a number of factors, including geographic location. According to the American Foundation for Suicide Prevention, in 2014 the ten US states with the highest suicide rates among all ages were (in descending order) Montana, Alaska, New Mexico, Wyoming, Utah, Idaho, Colorado, Nevada, Oklahoma, and Oregon. In Montana, on average one person commits suicide every thirty-five hours. In Alaska, suicide is the number one cause of death for youth aged fifteen to twenty-four. In New Mexico, more than three times as many people die by suicide each year as by homicide; in Wyoming, five times as many people die by

Native American Youth

The suicide rate among Native American youth has reached a crisis level, according to the CDC. A 2015 report published by the NCHS, a division of the CDC, shows that suicide rates among Native Americans are very different from those of the general population. Nationally, the highest suicide rate is among those who are white and middle-aged, but for Native Americans 40 percent of suicides are among those aged fifteen to twenty-four. There is great variation in this rate among the different Native American tribes, however. Some tribes have a youth suicide rate that is three times the national average; others may have a rate that is ten times the average.

The lead author of the report, Arialdi Miniño, cautions that the data are not always accurate, because some people who identify as Native American may not be listed as such on their death certificate. Therefore, he says, the number of Native American suicides given in the NCHS report is likely much lower than the actual figure. One reason for the high suicide rate is the high levels of unemployment and poverty among Native Americans living on reservations, which often leads to a sense of despair. Another explanation has to do with availability of mental health care. Mental illness such as depression plays a role in the vast majority of suicides, according to the National Alliance on Mental Illness. But mental health care is often in short supply among Native American communities.

suicide as by homicide each year; and in Utah, nine times as many people die by suicide as by homicide each year. All ten of these states have rates that are well above the national average. In fact, in Montana, which has the highest suicide rate in the United States, the rate is twice that of the national average.

The risk of teen suicide may also be tied to differences between rural and urban areas. According to a 2015 study published in *JAMA Pediatrics*, rural youth in the United States commit suicide at twice the rate of urban youth. This holds true for both boys and girls. The study examined data from more than sixty-six thousand youths aged ten to twenty-four who committed suicide in the United States from 1996 to 2010 and found that the gap between the rural and urban suicide rates grew significantly during that time frame. The researchers suggest this may be due to a number of reasons, including the fact that teens living in rural areas have less access to mental health services than teens who live in urban areas. In fact, more than half of rural communities in the United States lack access to a local mental health worker such as a psychiatrist or psychologist. In addition, rural teens may experience more stigma about seeking help for mental health issues, since self-reliance tends to be seen as a virtue in rural areas, according to the researchers. Lastly, teens in rural communities tend to have freer access to guns than urban teens, and the researchers suggest that it is no coincidence that youth in rural areas are more likely to choose a gun to commit suicide.

The risk of suicide varies by race and ethnicity, as well. Although suicide affects people of all races and ethnicities, some groups have higher suicide rates than others. According to the American Foundation for Suicide Prevention, in 2014 the highest suicide rate in the United States was among whites, with a rate of 14.7 suicides per 100,000 people. This was followed by American Indians and Alaska Natives, each with a rate of 10.9. The lowest suicide rates in the United States tend to be among Hispanics (6.3), Asians and Pacific Islanders (5.9), and African Americans (5.5).

Differences by Sex

There are also significant differences in the teen suicide rates of boys and girls. These differences can be seen in the results of the Youth Risk Behavior Survey (YRBS), which is conducted every two years by the CDC to monitor health risk behaviors of adolescents that contribute to death, disability, and social problems. The YRBS consists of a questionnaire that is given to a representative sample of thousands of ninth- through twelfth-grade students throughout the United States. The most recent YRBS, which was conducted in 2015, indicates that girls tend to report feelings of depression and thoughts of suicide at about twice the rate of boys. During the twelve months before the survey, 39.8 percent of girls and 20.3 percent of boys felt sad or hopeless almost every day for at least two weeks in a row. During the same time span, 23.4 percent of girls reported seriously considering attempting suicide, versus 12.2 percent of boys. Similarly, 19.4 percent of girls reported making a plan for how they would commit suicide, versus 9.8 percent of boys.

Girls also attempt suicide at more than twice the rate of boys. In the twelve months prior to the 2015 YRBS, 11.6 percent of girls reported making one or more suicide attempts, versus only 5.5 percent of boys. However, although the rate of attempted suicide is much higher for girls than for boys, boys are still much more likely to be successful in their attempts. In fact, boys commit suicide at three times the rate of girls, according to the NCHS. This disparity is largely due to the means chosen by boys and girls to take their lives. Girls who attempt suicide are more likely to try overdosing on pills or cutting themselves. Experts theorize that girls may choose to overdose because it is less violent and more dramatic, which allows them to "stage" their death. In contrast, boys are more likely to choose more violent means of committing suicide—especially firearms, which are more lethal, and much faster than overdosing. Boys are also more likely to jump from a high place or hang themselves than are girls. Such violent and lethal methods offer less chance of being rescued than a drug overdose, which means the boys are more likely to die in a suicide attempt; by the time someone discovers them, it is too late to prevent their death.

Most Common Methods

According to the CDC, the three most common methods used in suicide deaths of teens of either sex are firearms, poisoning (such as overdosing on pills or swallowing pesticides), and suffocation (which includes hanging and strangulation). Firearms are the most common means of suicide among teen boys, whereas overdosing is the most common method among teen girls. However, despite these differences between the two sexes, firearms remain the top method of suicide among all teens; according to the CDC, roughly 45 percent of teens who succeed in their suicide attempt

Girls attempt suicide more often than boys, but boys more often succeed in these attempts. The reason has to do with the methods used: Boys usually choose more lethal methods of suicide than girls do.

choose this method. Suffocation is the second-most common method among all teens and is used by about 40 percent. Poisoning is chosen by roughly 8 percent of all teens.

Among teens who attempt suicide but are unsuccessful, overdosing on pills is the most common method used. The reason for this, according to experts, is that it is easier to save a life by pumping a stomach than by repairing a gunshot wound.

The fact that firearms are the most common means of death among teens whose suicide attempts are successful is no coincidence, because they offer so little chance for rescue. In fact, according to the American Academy of Pediatrics (AAP), more than 90 percent of teens who attempt suicide with a firearm are successful in their attempt. Tragically, most of the guns used by teens to commit suicide belonged to a family member. This is a cause of great concern; according to the AAP, studies show that the risk of suicide is four to ten times higher in homes with guns than in those without. And even when gun owners are vigilant about access to their firearms and ammunition, this may not be enough to prevent a firearm-related suicide. In Colin Fraley's case his parents had stored their unloaded gun and all ammunition in separate places, out of their children's reach, but Colin used a chair to climb to the top shelf of the closet where the gun was stored and managed to load the weapon himself. According to the AAP, "Firearms in the home, regardless of whether they are kept unloaded or stored locked up, are associated with a higher risk for adolescent suicide."[18] The AAP therefore recommends that parents of teens at risk for suicide remove all firearms and ammunition from the house.

> "Firearms in the home, regardless of whether they are kept unloaded or stored locked up, are associated with a higher risk for adolescent suicide."[18]
>
> —The American Academy of Pediatrics

Suffocation is another commonly used suicide method among teens. According to the NCHS, its use as a suicide method has increased in recent years for both males and females of all ages. The NCHS also reports that from 1999 to 2014, for both males and females, suicide by firearm and drug overdose decreased, while suicide by suffocation increased. In 1999 fewer than one in five suicides in the general population were attributable to suffocation, whereas by 2014 the rate was about one in four.

The rise in the use of suffocation as a suicide method among teens is a troubling trend; as with firearms, a suicide attempt using suffocation is usually lethal. Experts are not certain what is behind the rise in suffocation suicides. Says Thomas Simon, a suicide expert with the CDC, "The data don't allow us to determine why."[19]

Regardless of the method used, when a teen makes the desperate decision to end his or her emotional turmoil by committing suicide, it is an unspeakable tragedy. Such a decision has devastating consequences for youths—and for their friends and families.

CHAPTER TWO

Why Do Teens Commit Suicide?

For fifteen-year-old Melanie, being on her high school's swim team was one of the best things in her life. But when her family moved to a new neighborhood, Melanie soon found her entire world turned upside down. There were so many changes in her life all at once that she had difficulty adjusting. "We switched schools, switched houses. I moved from an easy swim team to a really competitive one, it was just really overwhelming," she recalls. To top it off, she started dating a boy from school who became physically abusive toward her. One night Melanie decided to put an end to her unbearable stress by killing herself. "I left a note buried on my computer," she says. "I really just wrote it because I thought that's what you do when you commit suicide, but I didn't have anything to say."[20] Then she went to her father's medicine cabinet and swallowed countless pills she found there. Melanie survived her attempt because when her parents came to wake her for dinner, she told them she had taken the pills. They rushed her to the emergency room, and she remained hospitalized for a week and a half, during which she underwent a psychiatric evaluation and attended therapy sessions.

There is no single reason why teens decide to take their own lives. What causes an adolescent to commit suicide may be different from one teen to the next. "We don't know for sure [why some teens kills themselves], because when youth die by suicide they take the answers with them,"[21] says the Youth Suicide Prevention Program, which works to reduce teen suicide. The decision to commit suicide often involves some or all of these: mental, emotional, social, and academic issues. Each of these factors affects different teens in different ways, and some kids are better equipped to handle the various pressures and turmoil of life than others.

However, there are some common reasons behind suicide. According to the Substance Abuse and Mental Health Services Administration (SAMHSA), "While the events that lead to a suicide attempt can vary from person to person, a common theme that many suicide attempt survivors report is the need to feel relief. At desperate moments, when it feels like nothing else is working, suicide may seem like the only way to get relief from unbearable emotional pain."[22]

Depression and Suicide

The Youth Suicide Prevention Program explains that teens who commit suicide "are often experiencing a number of stressors and feel that they do not have the strength or desire to continue living. We also believe that the majority of youth who die by suicide have a mental disorder, like depression."[23] Depression does not always lead to suicide; millions of people—teens and adults—experience various shades of depression without ever trying to kill themselves. Nonetheless, depression is the primary cause of suicide in both youth and adults. Depression that leads a person to thoughts of suicide is a more serious type of depression than the normal "blues" of daily life. Clinical depression is a mood disorder in which the person feels overwhelming sadness, hopelessness, and despair for weeks or months on end. According to the AACAP, about 5 percent of children and teens in the United States suffer from clinical depression at any given time. In addition, children and teens who have experienced a loss, are under stress, have a family history of depression, or have learning or anxiety disorders are at higher risk for developing depression.

Signs of clinical depression in teens can include irritability, focusing on gloomy song lyrics, frequent school absences, poor or slipping grades, a loss of interest in activities that were formerly enjoyable, talking or writing about suicide or death, and giving away treasured belongings. Teens who are depressed may have a bleak outlook on life and make comments about the future being hopeless or things never getting better. They may also have difficulty sleeping—or conversely, they may sleep much more than usual. Either way, sleep disturbances can cause fatigue, anxiety, and irritability, which can in turn make the depression worse. And insomnia can actually increase suicidal thoughts and actions in those who suffer from it.

For teens who have never before experienced such symptoms, it may be difficult to recognize that they are suffering from depression. For example, when Melanie Demoree first began

Depression affects every aspect of daily life, including sleep patterns. Lack of sleep can worsen depression and increase suicidal thoughts.

feeling inner turmoil at age twelve, she did not understand what was happening to her. Demoree recalls:

> In middle school I started struggling with depression and, at the time, I didn't know what that was. I wasn't familiar with mental illness at all. So it was very lonely and I was kind of overwhelmed with a sense of hopelessness and worthlessness and not really wanting to live, and really having no reason to [feel that way]. I grew up with a great family and good friends and I never had any big, traumatic experiences or anything, which I'm grateful for, so I always felt kind of guilty for feeling that way.[24]

Demoree's feelings of depression and hopelessness spiraled out of control when she was in high school, to the point that she attempted suicide during her senior year. She says, "The reason I made my suicide attempt was 'cause I was just in such immense pain that I felt was too much to handle and I thought that was the only way out. I thought that the world would be better off without me."[25]

Depression and the Teen Brain

Experts know that an underlying reason people become depressed has to do with the brain's chemistry. The human brain contains cells that pass messages along from one to the other via chemicals known as neurotransmitters. The amount of neurotransmitters must be sufficient for the cells to do their job. When there is a decrease or imbalance in the amount of neurotransmitters, the cells cannot pass messages along correctly. Specifically, when the neurotransmitters serotonin and norepinephrine get out of balance due to chronic stress or anxiety, depression may result.

Complicating matters for teenagers is the state of their brains: The brains of adolescents are in a state of flux. They are developing throughout adolescence and even into early adulthood. Be-

Bullying Leads Teen to Thoughts of Suicide

Joe Taraszka describes how being bullied in high school led him to become suicidal:

In seventh grade three other boys made my life a misery. At nutrition and lunch, they chased me around the school. When they caught me, they'd push me around and say anything to demean me (which didn't take a whole lot). It wasn't limited to school. They also got my home phone number and started crank-calling me.

A few times I tried to fight back at school, but since I had never hit anything in my life, it was pointless the second I put up my fists. One day I picked up a board to defend myself. A teacher saw me and called me over. I thought maybe she'd help me. Crying, I told her all the pain they had made me feel. But when she talked to them, they twisted everything around and made me seem like a bad guy. They were let off and nothing changed. It made me feel like I couldn't count on anyone to help me.

After that, I used to sit in my room and plan what to put in my will. I'd blame my death on the three bullies. I imagined my own funeral, wondering who would show up. I didn't think anyone would come.

Things got worse in high school. . . . I was afraid of other kids and sat like a rock at my desk, hoping no one would make fun of me.

Joe Taraszka, "My Struggle with Depression," *L.A. Youth*, May–June 2003. www.layouth.com.

cause of this, teen thinking is not always rational. The Society for the Prevention of Teen Suicide explains:

Lots of people think about suicide at one time or another in their lives, teens included. Usually it's because they're struggling with problems in their lives that seem overwhelming, and they feel trapped, helpless, and hopeless. It isn't that they want to die—they just want to stop feeling miserable. They may be depressed, angry, or empty—but whatever they feel, they're not thinking clearly.[26]

Part of the reason teens may not think clearly about their problems or their decision to attempt suicide is that the brain's frontal lobe, which is responsible for problem solving, judgment, and impulse control, is not fully developed until adulthood. "It's the irrational thinking in suicide that makes it so complex for us to understand," says Maureen Underwood, clinical director for the Society for the Prevention of Teen Suicide. "Many kids do not understand that once they're dead, they're dead forever. They don't understand the finality of it."[27]

The Importance of Risk Factors

Experts believe the likelihood of a teen turning to suicide may be influenced by risk factors. Major depression is one of the biggest of these risk factors, but there are others. And the possibility of suicide is greatly increased when a teen experiences several risk factors at the same time. In addition to depression, substance abuse is a major risk factor for suicide. SAMHSA reports that alcohol and drug abuse can increase the risk of suicide as much as six times. Another risk factor is violent and impulsive behavior. Teens who have trouble controlling their anger may act on an aggressive impulse by harming or killing themselves. Another factor that can place a depressed teen at higher risk of suicide is a past suicide attempt. "It does not matter how long ago a person attempted suicide; if someone attempted it once, he or she is more likely to attempt it again, no matter how many years have elapsed,"[28] says psychiatrist William Coryell.

One big risk factor for suicide, especially for teens, is relationship troubles. Some teens may become depressed after a breakup with a romantic partner, for example, and may slip into such a state of despair that they begin to consider suicide. Police believe this is what happened in the case of sixteen-year-old Jaylin Loredo of San Antonio, Texas. Loredo had been despondent over a recent breakup with her boyfriend and had sent him suicidal text messages. She was found unconscious in the parking lot of a local fire station one evening in July 2016, and paramedics were unable to revive her. Police believe she killed herself by overdosing on pills.

Additional risk factors for suicide include a family history of suicide; the death of a loved one; physical or sexual abuse; and lesbian, gay, bisexual, transgender, or questioning orientation identification. Teens who have one or more of these risk factors may have a hard time handling stressful events such as bullying—and they turn to suicide as a way out.

Bullying

Indeed, bullying is a common factor in teen suicide. Researchers at the University of Manchester in the United Kingdom studied data related to the suicides of 130 youths under age twenty that occurred between January 2014 and April 2015. The researchers were looking for common factors that may have led the young people to take their own lives. Their findings, which were published in the medical journal Lancet in 2016, indicated that bullying played a role in nearly one-fourth (22 percent) of the suicides. In many cases the bullying had taken place in the past, but some of the teens had been bullied within three months of their suicide.

This was the case for fourteen-year-old Destiny Gleason of Warrenton, Missouri, who had been bullied for several months before committing suicide in April 2016. According to her mother, the problem started the previous fall, when Destiny entered a new school after the family moved to Warrenton. Several of Destiny's new classmates began relentlessly bullying her at school. "At one point they took some photo of some random person's private parts and put Destiny's name across it and spread it around the school," her mother said. "Anything they could possibly do to hurt her and bring her down."[29] The final straw came when the bullies posted several mean-spirited comments about Destiny on Facebook; after reading the postings, Destiny went into her bedroom and hanged herself.

Teens who are subjected to relentless cyberbullying often feel they have no way to escape. Desperate for a way out, and finding no other form of relief, some of these teens have killed themselves.

Other teens who have been bullied or cyberbullied have reacted in ways similar to Destiny Gleason. One example is fifteen-year-old Tovonna Holton, a high school freshman in Florida. In June 2016 Holton discovered that cyberbullies had filmed a nude video of her without her knowledge or permission and posted the video on Snapchat. Hours after her discovery, Holton was so horrified by the extreme violation that she took a gun from her mother's purse, went into a bathroom in her family's home, and fatally shot herself.

Researchers, as well as the general public, are becoming increasingly aware of the devastating consequences of teen bullying. According to child psychiatrist Benjamin Shain, lead author of an AAP report titled "Suicide and Suicide Attempts in Adolescents" in the June 2016 edition of *Pediatrics*, "Bullying has always been a major issue for adolescents, but there is now greater recognition of the connection between bullying and suicide. The Internet is a key influence, as well. Cyberbullying, for example, is as serious a problem as face-to-face bullying."[30]

Suicide as an Option

The suicide of a friend, classmate, or family member can also put teens at risk because they now see suicide as an option. This can lead to what are called suicide clusters—multiple suicides taking place in close succession in the same location. There are about five teen suicide clusters in the United States each year.

Researchers from the Harvard School of Public Health and the Canadian universities of Ottawa and Alberta investigated the theory that suicide can be "contagious." In a study that was published in 2013 in the *Canadian Medical Association Journal*, the researchers surveyed thousands of teenagers about the effects of suicide by a friend or schoolmate. "Adolescents may be particularly susceptible to this contagion effect,"[31] the researchers state. The study found that more than 13 percent of teen suicides can be explained by clustering. More than 24 percent of the sixteen- to seventeen-year-old respondents said a schoolmate of theirs had committed suicide, with 20 percent reporting they knew someone personally who had done so. Researchers compared the level of suicidal thinking among those who had been exposed to a schoolmate's suicide within the past year and found it was much higher than for those who were not exposed. For example, among the sixteen- and seventeen-year-olds, the rate was more than twice as high for those exposed to a suicide as it was for those who were not exposed. And for that same age group, attempted suicides were three times higher among those exposed to a suicide than for those not exposed. The researchers suggest the effects on teens of exposure to the suicide of another can last at least two years.

Suicide contagion can also play a role in suicide pacts and copycat suicides. Some troubled teens may make an agreement to commit suicide together. Police suspect this was the case with Texas teens Ritu Sachdeva and Hillary Kate Kuizon, who both attended Plano East Senior High School and committed suicide within hours of each other in February 2016. A more common phenomenon among teens, however, is the copycat suicide, in which teens imitate the suicide method of others. According to a 2014 study in *Lancet Psychiatry*, when a young adult commits suicide, a spike in teen copycat suicides follows; the more sensational and prominent the media reports are, the larger the spike. According to Madelyn Gould, author of the study, teens are nearly four times as likely to commit a copycat suicide as any other age group. "It just seems so frightening, but a lot of behaviors are modeled,"[32] says Gould. She says a likely reason for this modeling is based in social learning theory—that is, when vulnerable teens are going through issues similar to a recent suicide victim, they are more likely to view suicide as a solution.

Academic Pressures

Another factor that can serve as a trigger for teen suicide is the pressure to succeed in school, both academically and athletically. Academic pressures on teens, including schoolwork, grades, and planning for the future (such as applying for college or getting a job) can cause a great deal of stress. In the 2016 University of Manchester study of the suicides of 130 young people under age twenty, researchers found that just over one-fourth (27 percent) were experiencing school-related pressure and anxiety. "Academic pressures, especially related to exams, were common, although often unrecognized at the time, and four deaths occurred on the day of an exam or the day after,"[33] the researchers wrote.

Bryce Goldsen, a junior at Bishop Blanchet, a Catholic high school near Seattle, Washington, is no stranger to such school-related pressure and stress. He plays varsity tennis and takes advanced placement history and language arts classes, all while maintaining a grade point average near 4.0. But Goldsen admits he is frequently stressed-out. "Most of my stress comes from the pressure to perform well day in and day out,"[34] he says. For Gold-

LGBTQ at Risk

One group of teens that is at particularly high risk of suicide due to bullying are those who are lesbian, gay, bisexual, transgender, or questioning their sexual identity (LGBTQ). This was the case for sixteen-year-old Adam Kizer of Sonoma, California. Kizer, who was bisexual, had been bullied since childhood. "I don't think the boy went a whole week without somebody messing with him," says his father. "They would tell him 'You should kill yourself.'" As a consequence of the bullying, Kizer suffered from depression and tried to kill himself several times. In the spring of 2015, Kizer took his own life by hanging himself at his grandmother's home.

When Leelah Alcorn came out as transgender at age fourteen to her parents, they refused to accept her female identity. Instead, her parents put her in a conversion therapy program in an effort to make her accept the male gender assigned to her at birth. In 2014 the seventeen-year-old Alcorn committed suicide by stepping in front of a semitrailer. In her suicide note, Alcorn wrote that she killed herself because her parents were never going to accept her transgender identity. "Please don't be sad, it's for the better," she wrote. "The life I would've lived isn't worth living in . . . because I'm transgender. . . . To put it simply, I feel like a girl trapped in a boy's body."

Quoted in Darren Wee, "Bisexual Teen Commits Suicide After Years of Severe Bullying," Gay Star News, June 4. 2015. www.gaystarnews.com.

Quoted in Ashley Frantz, "An Ohio Transgender Teen's Suicide, a Mother's Anguish," CNN, January 4, 2015. www .cnn.com.

sen the stress provides a motivation to do even better in school. But other teens are not able to handle the stress and anxiety of such pressure in such a positive way.

Indeed, the pressure some kids feel to excel in school can be overwhelming. An example of this is Taylor Chiu, who attempted suicide as a high school freshman in California because of pressures to excel academically and athletically. Chiu grew up in a family that expected her and her brother to work hard and perform well in school. She and her brother were picked up from school every day by their mother, who kept tabs on their homework assignments, upcoming tests, and grades. Chiu and her brother were expected to finish their homework before they could play, and they would never have even thought of going to bed at night without finishing the next day's school assignment. Chiu appreciated her parents' involvement in her schoolwork, but by the time she was in high school, the pressure to succeed began to be too much for her. During her freshman year, she was a Girl Scout, joined the swim team, played trombone in the school jazz band, and was chosen for a role in a school play. She began her days at six o'clock in the morning with an hour's swim before school. After school she went to swim practice and then rehearsed for the play until seven o'clock at night, when she returned home to study. She also squeezed in band practices and Girl Scout meetings during the week. Her parents and teachers were very proud of her, but Chiu was stressed-out and very tired. "I was exhausted to the bone," she recalls. "I remember just not being happy about anything, and I just couldn't make it slow down. And I thought there would never be any escape."[35]

> "I remember just not being happy about anything, and I just couldn't make it slow down. And I thought there would never be any escape."[35]
>
> —Taylor Chiu, who attempted suicide when she was a freshman in high school

Then something happened when she was fifteen that sparked a deep depression: She got an F on a geometry test. The pressures placed on her by her parents and teachers to excel at school, both academically and athletically, became too much for her to handle. Her depression and sleep deprivation combined to make it difficult for her to think clearly, and she began to dwell on thoughts of harming herself. Then one night after swim practice, she swallowed an entire bottle of Advil. "I was in pain and I wanted a way out of my pain," she recalls. "I wanted a break from my relentless schedule. I wanted people to notice that I was suffering."[36] Fortunately for Chiu, her brother noticed she was acting strangely and alerted their parents, who found the empty bottle of Advil and rushed her to the hospital. She spent several days in the hospital but survived.

Reasons Not Always Clear

The factors that lead a person to take his or her own life are numerous and complex, and there is still much that experts do not know about why kids commit suicide. In Taylor Chiu's case, her family knows exactly what drove her to the attempt on her life, because she survived to talk about it. But for those who do not survive a suicide attempt and do not leave a note, the reasons for their desperate actions are not always so clear.

This was the case with seventeen-year-old Harry Lee, a high school senior in Palo Alto, California. After struggling with depression for several weeks, he committed suicide in January 2015 by jumping from a high building. But Lee did not tell anyone of his plans or leave an explanation for his actions. His mother, Kathleen, is resigned to never really knowing or understanding why he took his own life. And she says that many other people who lose a loved one to suicide may never fully understand what brought them to commit that terrible and desperate final act. "They are not robots," she says. "You can't break them open and find the broken circuit. It's so complicated. There is so much you don't know, and you are never going to know. . . . We are not going to have 'the answer.' We will just do our best."[37]

CHAPTER THREE

What Is It Like to Live with Suicidal Feelings?

Feelings of sadness are a normal part of life—especially when a person (whatever their age) experiences a loss or some other painful event. But when sadness persists, when it turns into despair or hopelessness, and when these feelings seem utterly unmanageable, this is when thoughts of suicide sometimes arise. Teens who have reached this point—teens who have attempted suicide but survived—can help others understand the feelings and thoughts that brought them to that moment in their lives.

No Light at the End of the Tunnel

Depression can be a debilitating experience, one that takes the joy out of a person and makes the simplest actions of daily life seem insurmountable. Rebecca Perkins, author of *Words of Wisdom for My 24 Year Old: A Parenting Manifesto*, experienced profound depression as a teen. She recalls what it was like:

> Depression is not about feeling sad. It is not about feeling a bit down or being in a bad mood. Depression is a blackness. Depression sucks all emotion from you. You are left feeling hollow and numb and with a deep sense of hopelessness and loneliness. Depression drains the world of color and sound and taste and smell. I have experienced some very black and bleak places in my mind. I spent some of my teenage years with depression. . . . There were days when I could barely get out of bed.[38]

People who live with these feelings sometimes cannot see the light at the end of the proverbial tunnel. Teens, in particular, often do not have the life experience to realize that their situation will improve—that things will get better. This was the case for Amanda Redhead, a registered nurse who attempted suicide as a teen. At the time she could not envision her depression ever lifting. Redhead explains, "When I was 17 years old, I was swimming in the black water of a deep, dark depression—a depression that I could not ever see myself coming out of and in those dark days I tried to blot out my own life several times. . . . During those very dark days . . . I felt terribly alone and was sure that living in this unspeakable pain forever would be my destiny."[39] Kristen Anderson, author of *Life, in Spite of Me*, also attempted suicide as a teen because she felt that her depression would never lift. She says that a series of events led her into a downward spiral of despair. Within the space of two years, three of her friends and her beloved grandmother died. Soon after these tragedies, Anderson was raped by an acquaintance. She became depressed and deeply despondent, and at age seventeen she attempted to end her own life. "I just started to think life was horrible—this world was horrible, and I was going to be miserable the rest of my life," Anderson recalls. "I started to become a lot more introverted, I think at this point. When people would ask me how I was doing, like if I came into work or something at school, I would be like, 'I'm here. Isn't that good enough?' I started to just lose hope."[40]

> "Depression drains the world of color and sound and taste and smell. I have experienced some very black and bleak places in my mind. . . . There were days when I could barely get out of bed."[38]
>
> —Rebecca Perkins, author of *Words of Wisdom for My 24 Year Old: A Parenting Manifesto*

One of the most debilitating aspects of depression is the feeling of losing control of one's own life. Taylor Chiu, who survived a suicide attempt at age fifteen and today is a motivational speaker, recalls, "I've heard depression described as a prison, a hole, a jacket, a weight. An entrapment that you fall into, a force that controls you. I have felt all of these things. As a young person with undiagnosed depression, I felt completely trapped by a life that I hadn't chosen. I felt I had no control over my daily routine, schoolwork, extracurriculars, or social identity."[41] Chiu says that it was the feeling that she had lost all control over her life that led her to attempt suicide.

Apathy and Loss of Interest

One outgrowth of depression that can feed suicidal feelings is apathy—which is a lack of interest, feeling, and emotion. Psychologist Carl E. Pickhardt calls the link between apathy and depression "a vicious cycle." He explains, "Depression can breed apathy, and apathy can sustain depression."[42] Many teens who are depressed and suicidal become apathetic; they simply stop caring about things that once mattered to them. This can lead them to neglect themselves, their friends, and their schoolwork. Some depressed teens even stop caring about their own personal hygiene. Ordinary things like brushing their teeth or bathing become an onerous chore. Karen A., a teen who suffered from depression, explains the effect that apathy had on her:

> I stopped caring about everything. I distracted myself by reading and watching TV. I even stopped showering. I could smell myself and my hair was greasy. After a while I noticed dark patches on my skin. I rubbed it and the dead skin came off. I realized the dark patches were dirt. Eww. I washed my arms in the sink or in the pool. Looking back, it grosses me out that I didn't shower but I can understand because I was depressed and I didn't feel like doing anything.[43]

Some teens who are locked into the apathy of depression may drop out of clubs or sports, for example, because they no longer enjoy or care about these activities. According to the AACAP, "A child who used to play often with friends may now spend most of the time alone and without interests. Things that were once fun now bring little joy to the depressed child."[44] Typi-

Teens who are depressed and thinking about suicide often lose interest in the things that once mattered to them. Favorite sports, school, friends, and hobbies may no longer have any appeal.

cal is the story of sixteen-year-old Ian Hartley of Charlotte, Michigan, who killed himself in 2016. Hartley had been an active teen who played on the Charlotte High School varsity soccer team and also loved skateboarding around his neighborhood. He was a good student and was well liked by his classmates. And he had a close and loving relationship with his parents and his siblings. His mother recalls, "He was just one of those kids that was, you

Arthur Curtis's Story

Teen Arthur Curtis explains his experience with depression and suicidal feelings as a high school senior:

It was difficult even to think during those days, I just sat and stared off into space for the longest time in and out of class. I felt utterly useless, and that, no matter how hard I tried, I would never be able to do anything right.

I was completely overwhelmed by everything that was going on, all at once. It felt like nobody really knew or cared just how difficult it was for me personally to handle all of that pressure all at once. I was never really given a choice about what to do. . . . It made me realize, that if this is what was going to be, what the rest of my life was going to be like, then I didn't want to grow up.

I felt trapped, and that things were happening to me and my life that were out of my control. To me, it didn't even seem like I was even living a life, to the point where I felt like committing suicide wouldn't even really be "suicide."

Arthur Curtis, e-mail message to author, August 8, 2016.

know, just a good, all-American kind of kid."[45] But one evening in early 2016, Hartley confided in his mother that he was feeling depressed. Over the next few weeks, he became more and more withdrawn, often returning home from school to go straight to his room, close the door, and go to sleep. His teachers noticed that he would stare blankly into space during class, and his grades began to slip. Hartley soon lost all interest in the activities he used to find enjoyable, and he eventually dropped out of the school soccer team.

As depression and apathy grow, staying engaged with family, friends, classmates, and teachers becomes exceedingly difficult—almost impossible. Joe Taraszka, who says he became suicidal in high school, explains his struggle to remain engaged while in the throes of depression:

I felt like the world was slowly fading away. My body was slow and heavy as if I was walking on the bottom of a pool. Just lifting up my hand to write my name was a chore that required much concentration. When I spoke, I felt like my words had to break down walls, and even then I couldn't properly relate to anyone. Everything lost meaning. It's like I was watching the world on the silver screen while I sat in the back row.[46]

An Impulse to Escape

Many teens who attempt suicide are not actually thinking about death or wanting to die—rather, they are trying to escape what feels to them like unbearable pain. Experts say this is borne out by interviews with young people who have attempted suicide. Many of these young people have said they only wanted to find some way out of an impossible situation or to relieve feelings that tormented them. One man whose daughter attempted suicide during her senior year of high school describes his daughter's comments when she was well enough to speak: "She did not think of suicide when she did this, she just did not want to feel any more pain, physical or emotional."[47]

This is exactly how Megan Rotatori felt when she attempted suicide at age seventeen. She says she reached a point in her depression where she realized "I can't live like this anymore." She says the reason she tried to take her own life was because "even on a day to day basis, I was just underlyingly miserable. There was always this underlying mood. I just was unhappy. I didn't want to live like that, either. It wasn't just the ups and downs of those really, really low moods—[it was] just the everyday wearing on me, not ever being able to be 100% happy."[48]

Kristen Anderson, too, was trying to escape overwhelming emotional turmoil when she tried to end her life. "The pain that I

> "I felt like the world was slowly fading away. . . . Everything lost meaning. It's like I was watching the world on the silver screen while I sat in the back row."[46]
>
> —Joe Taraszka, who struggled with thoughts of suicide while in high school

felt inside simply overwhelmed me, and I didn't think I could take it anymore,"[49] she says. One night as she was walking home from a friend's house and feeling extremely depressed, she passed by some railroad tracks. "Right before [the train] got there, I made the impulsive decision to lay down on the tracks," she recalls. "I wanted the pain to end. I just wanted it to be over."[50] She was run over by thirty-three freight cars and survived, but she lost both her legs and must now use a wheelchair.

On the night Anderson decided to commit suicide, it was a split-second choice. Many other teens who are overwhelmed by their emotional struggles also make the impulsive decision to commit suicide. According to the *New England Journal of Medicine*, up to 80 percent of all suicide attempts are carried out on an impulse, with 70 percent taking less than an hour between the decision and the actual attempt. Many of those who are fortunate enough to survive this impulsive decision say they regretted their actions. Kevin Hines is in this group. He made an impulsive decision at age eighteen to commit suicide by jumping from the Golden Gate Bridge in San Francisco and says that he regretted his action the moment he jumped: "My first thought was, 'What the hell did I just do? I don't want to die.'"[51]

Hiding Their Feelings

After a suicide, it is not uncommon for friends and family to say they did not realize the depth of despair being experienced by the person who committed the act. There is a good reason for this. People who are considering suicide, including teens, often hide their feelings from those they care about. In some instances they may be unable to find the right words or the right time to express their feelings. One teen who became suicidal in high school recalls, "In the face of friends, I would always fake joyous emotions so that they wouldn't know my pain, so that I wouldn't have to try explaining just how I felt."[52]

Some teens may keep their suicidal feelings inside because they do not want to upset their family and friends. One example is seventeen-year-old Brittany Corcoran, who had been severely depressed since age fourteen and killed herself in 2016. During the years before her suicide, her family says, she kept the depths of her inner struggles to herself. Her parents believe she hid the extent of her sadness and despair to spare her loved ones from anguish. Although Corcoran was in counseling, she "got better at hiding, hiding it all and not making people worry about her,"[53] according to her mother.

Other teens may not tell anyone about their depression because they feel like no one will understand them. They may not even fully understand their own feelings. When Jordan Burnham became suicidal at age sixteen, he says he "felt like there was still a hole inside of me, and I couldn't figure out why I had a lack of motivation to get out of bed, why I was randomly crying. So when I was 16, I was going to school with a mask on my face, acting and pretending as though I was really happy with the things that were going on around me."[54]

In addition, some teens may be afraid of what might happen to them if they confess they are feeling suicidal. They may fear others will think they are insane and lock them up. Burnham also said, "When I had these suicidal thoughts, I didn't know how to talk to anyone because I figured I was the only one who had those thoughts and emotions and if I told someone, I just figured that the automatic reaction would be I'd have to go to a psych ward."[55]

> "One of the things I hate the most is the stereotype of 'crazy,' 'psychotic,' or whatever, 'cause I have definitely been called that by some people."[56]
>
> —Megan Rotatori, who attempted suicide at age seventeen

Living with Stigma and Shame

Experts say that the reason suicidal teens fear what others might think of them is because depression—indeed, any mental illness—is stigmatized in US culture. Many people hold negative attitudes about mental illness, viewing it as something disgraceful or even frightening. Megan Rotatori, who attempted suicide at age seventeen, says, "One of the things I hate the most is the stereotype of 'crazy,' 'psychotic,' or whatever, 'cause I have definitely been called that by some people."[56] Some teens who attempt suicide may try to hide their actions from others, including friends and parents. This was the case with Mike Woodard's teenage daughter, who overdosed on pain pills and then asked her sister to drive her to the emergency room in hopes that their parents would not find out she had attempted suicide.

In the aftermath of a suicide attempt, many teens may feel guilty or ashamed of their actions, and they may fear that friends and family members will judge them. Kate Wren of Toronto, Canada, who survived a suicide attempt at age sixteen, says that the next day she felt shame over her attempt, as well as "fear about how people would react. Would they be angry?"[57] The nurse at the hospital did not help matters much when she chastised Wren by telling her that she was taking up space in the emergency room that people who were truly sick needed.

Because of their feelings of guilt or shame, as well as their fear of what others may think or say about them, many teens choose to keep quiet about their suicidal thoughts or actions. Amanda Redhead, a registered nurse who survived several suicide attempts as a teen, says that the stigma associated with mental illness can make it difficult or even impossible for many teens to seek the help they need. "For every person brave enough to say that they struggle with depression, anxiety . . . there are likely hundreds more in the wings who are not ready yet to take the stage and come forward about their own struggles,"[58] says Redhead.

Long-Term Challenges

For most people depression does not simply just go away. It may even last a lifetime, but it can be managed with professional help. Managing depression does not mean that the stresses of life disappear—sometimes those stresses may still seem almost unbearable. Jordan Burnham says he does not consider suicide an option anymore, even in those moments when life feels incredibly challenging. "I have the same depression that I had before, but . . . I don't have thoughts of wanting to try and take my own life. Do I question, you know, how I am going to get through this day and why am I here? Yeah, I definitely have thoughts of that."[59]

Yet for many, thoughts of suicide do not easily fade. Experts say that once individuals have considered or attempted suicide, they are at higher risk of doing so again because it becomes part

High School Students Considering Suicide

Teens who feel they have no way out of depression or other difficult life challenges sometimes contemplate suicide as a solution. According to the 2015 Youth Risk Behavior Survey, conducted by the CDC, a large percentage of high school students have seriously considered killing themselves—and many of them have even come up with a plan for carrying out the act.

Percentage of High School Students Who Seriously Considered Attempting Suicide and Who Made a Plan About How They Would Attempt Suicide*

Race/Ethnicity	Seriously considered attempting suicide		Made a Suicide Plan	
	Female	Male	Female	Male
White	22.8%	11.5%	18.4%	9.3%
Black	18.7%	11%	17.3%	10.6%
Hispanic	25.6%	12.4%	20.7%	10.9%
Grade				
9	26.5%	10.7%	22.5%	8.1%
10	25.7%	10.8%	21.6%	9.2%
11	22.1%	13.3%	17.2%	10.4%
12	18.6%	14%	15.7%	12%

*During the twelve months before the survey.

Source: Centers for Disease Control and Prevention, "Youth Risk Behavior Surveillance—United States, 2015." *Morbidity and Mortality Weekly Report.* June 10, 2016. www.cdc.gov.

of their "menu" of choices. In fact, researchers have found that people who previously attempted suicide are more likely to eventually kill themselves than those with no prior attempts. One study conducted in Toronto, Canada, and published in *JAMA Psychiatry* in 2015, identified more than 65,000 people who had been hospitalized for a suicide attempt involving an intentional drug overdose over an eight-year time span; 18,500 of these were teens. The researchers found that the risk of suicide among those who had previously attempted suicide was forty-two times higher

Stacy Hollingsworth's Story

Stacy Hollingsworth shares her experiences with suicide and depression as a teen:

I used to think that depression and suicide were things that happened to other people, that the way I approached my life somehow prevented me from becoming a victim of mental illness. I realized just how incorrect that assumption was when my own life was turned upside down by major depression.

I first noticed that something was wrong in 8th grade. Apparently, so did one of my teachers, because she asked me if anything was wrong. Unfortunately, she did so in front of the whole class. From that day on, I put up a wall to protect myself from the embarrassment of having a stigmatized illness. I wore a mask—a façade—to cover up what I was actually going through. I didn't feel comfortable sharing my feelings with any adults in my life at that time.

My depression continued in high school. I was hoping that someone—anyone—would bring up the topics of depression and suicide, so that I wouldn't have to. In school, there were always lessons about alcohol, drugs, and safe sex—but never ONCE were depression or suicide mentioned. Maybe, just maybe, if the adults in my life had been educated in these topics, I would have felt comfortable asking for help, and I would have been spared years of suffering.

Stacy Hollingsworth, "A First-Person Message for Teens," Society for the Prevention of Teen Suicide, 2016. www.sptsusa.org.

than that of the general population. Furthermore, this risk could persist for many years. A total of 107 teens in the study who had survived their initial suicide attempt wound up taking their own lives on average just over two years later. And about one-fourth had committed suicide four years after being discharged from the hospital after their first attempt. "I think the key message is that patients at all ages—both teenagers and adults—who present to hospital with a first episode of intentional self-poisoning are at a significantly increased risk of suicide over the ensuing decade," says Yaron Finkelstein, lead author of the study. "The suicide risk is durable over many years."[60]

Candace Paige, who slipped into a major depression during her junior year in high school, is one who feels like her depression will always be with her and that she is likely to feel suicidal again in the future. Paige explains:

I first became suicidal at age sixteen. . . . The pain was so intense—my stomach churned all the time, my heart ached, and I did not want to go on living.

Somehow, I made it through that time. But my depression has returned again and again, and each time, my thoughts would slip back to that desperate place where I thought I would be better off dead. I even thought those around me would be better off without me in their lives, because I was just depressed and gloomy all the time. Every day, it seems like, I have to struggle with these thoughts. Do I deserve to be here, walking on this planet? Am I OK? Can I go on living today, or is my life not worth the effort? Honestly, some days, it's all I can do to hold myself together. Will I ever be fully OK? I wish I could say "yes," but the truth is, I just don't know.[61]

Living with Despair

Depressed teens live with despair day in and day out. Many feel stigmatized by their depression, and some try to hide their true feelings from others. Although most people who have survived suicide attempts regret their actions, the fact remains that they are now more likely to face the possibility of suicidal thoughts in the future.

Teens whose depression becomes so severe that they consider ending their lives are locked in a struggle that is almost beyond comprehension. "Most of us can hardly imagine the suffering that precedes suicide and the pain left in its wake," says Kay Redfield Jamison, a psychiatry professor at the Johns Hopkins University School of Medicine. "When the person who dies is young, the devastation is even more profound. . . . Suicide is a terrible killer of the young."[62]

CHAPTER FOUR

How Can Teen Suicide Be Prevented?

The terrible reality of suicide is that it cannot always be prevented. But often it can. Early and appropriate intervention can prevent a depressed teen from killing himself or herself. "Even the most severely depressed person has mixed feelings about death, wavering until the very last moment between wanting to live and wanting to die," says the Jason Foundation. "Most suicidal people do not want to die; they want the pain to stop. The impulse to end their life, however overpowering, does not last forever."[63]

Challenges of Treatment and Prevention

Recognizing the signs that someone may be experiencing extreme distress and suicidal thoughts is the first step in prevention. As simple as it sounds, that is not always easily accomplished. Many teens do not reveal their feelings, especially to the adults in their lives. And sometimes adults miss or misunderstand the cues they get from teens who may actually be trying to show their distress but not know how to go about it. Lack of understanding or recognition can get in the way of prevention efforts. Clinical psychologist Cheryl King is one of the nation's foremost authorities on youth and young-adult suicide risk assessment and prevention. She says one of the most significant barriers to teens getting the help they need is a lack of recognition: "Teens may be unaware that their problems are treatable, concerned about the stigma, [or] put off by the idea of needing help. The people around them also may not recognize a young person's problem as a treatable mental disorder."[64]

Even when family and friends see signs of distress in a teen, they do not always recognize it for what it is. The reason is this: Many of the signs of suicidal thinking—such as becoming withdrawn, crying a lot, exhibiting irritability, or engaging in risky behavior—are also common teen behaviors. "Many times, signs of concern mimic 'typical teenage behaviors,'" says the Jason Foundation. "So, how can we know if it's just 'being a teenager' or something more? If the signs are persisting over a period of time, several of the signs appear at the same time, and the behavior is 'out of character' for the young person as you know him/her, then close attention is warranted."[65]

There are some fairly obvious, unmistakable signs that a teen may be at imminent risk for committing suicide. These include talking about death or suicide, discussing a plan to commit suicide, or making a suicide attempt. Individuals who recognize these serious warning signs in others or in themselves should seek help.

> "Even the most severely depressed person has mixed feelings about death, wavering until the very last moment between wanting to live and wanting to die."[63]
>
> —The Jason Foundation, an organization that works to prevent teen suicide

Helping Someone in Crisis

When individuals suspect that a friend or sibling or other person they care about is thinking about suicide, there are ways to help. Experts stress that it is important to talk to the person about how he or she is feeling. Listening to the person and offering nonjudgmental support are also helpful. In addition, friends and family can encourage the person to talk to others, such as a school counselor, peer counselor, teacher, parent, or other trusted friend. "If a teen talks about wanting to end her life," says psychologist Lucie Hemmen, "even if she seems dramatic, take it seriously. Tell her you love her, you hear her, and you are committed to helping her through these feelings. Let her know that you believe she can get through this and that you are there for her."[66]

One quick and easy way to get help for a suicidal person is by calling a suicide prevention hotline. Such hotlines are staffed by people who are trained to help individuals of all ages who are in crisis. There are many local hotlines available throughout the nation. The National Suicide Prevention Lifeline has a nationwide, toll-free, confidential crisis line that is available twenty-four hours a day. It connects callers with a trained counselor at a crisis center in their area.

Some teens may not feel comfortable talking on the telephone, especially if they are feeling emotionally overwrought. But there are several other quick ways to get help in a crisis. For example, in addition to its crisis line, the National Suicide Prevention Lifeline website has a "Click to Chat" button available to individuals in crisis. Other examples include Crisis Text Line and Text-A-Tip, both of which provide free crisis intervention via text message. All of these methods provide a way for people of any age to reach a trained crisis counselor at any time of day or night.

If a suicide attempt appears likely, it is important not to leave the person alone. Friends or family members should remove any firearms, drugs, knives, or other objects that could be used in a suicide attempt. In an immediate crisis, if the person is actively suicidal and becoming a threat to his or her own safety, friends or family should transport the person to a hospital emergency room or call 911 to get help from a medical or mental health professional.

> "If a teen talks about wanting to end her life, even if she seems dramatic, take it seriously. . . . Let her know that you believe she can get through this and that you are there for her."[66]
>
> —Lucie Hemmen, a psychologist in Santa Cruz, California

Counseling Approaches

While hotlines and emergency services are warranted in an immediate crisis, they are not a replacement for longer-term inter-

A student talks with her school counselor about the difficulties she is experiencing. Experts say that talking to someone about one's feelings is the first and most important step in getting help.

ventions such as counseling. For long-term, ongoing help, various types of counseling are available. Research has shown that certain counseling approaches lead to a reduction in suicidal thoughts in teens.

One approach that has been successful with teens is cognitive behavioral therapy (CBT). This form of therapy is one of the most commonly used for those who are depressed or suicidal. CBT helps individuals recognize distorted or inaccurate thoughts, beliefs, and attitudes. Once they learn to spot these patterns, they can begin to change their behavior. One aspect of CBT involves helping people who have attempted suicide identify the thoughts and behaviors that preceded the attempt so that they are better able to seek intervention before attempting to harm

A Teacher Steps In to Help

Brittni Darras, a high school English teacher in Colorado, did not know why one of her students missed several weeks of school. She found out why when the student's mother came to a parent-teacher conference. The girl had deleted her accounts on social media, written letters to her closest friends and relatives, and tried to kill herself. Darras was deeply upset by this news. "She's beautiful," Darras said. "She has friends. She comes in class, and she's laughing. She's the top in my class, always has A's, always does the best job on the assignments. She's just a phenomenal, phenomenal human being. So I never would have guessed that she was struggling."

Darras decided to take action. She wanted each of her students to know that she cares about them. She spent about two months composing handwritten notes to all 130 of her students and handed out the notes after final exams. One of the notes read, "I hope you know how special you are to me. You inspire me to be a better person every day." One student was so moved that she said she planned to keep the note forever, and every student gave Darras a hug on the way out of the classroom.

Quoted in Sarah Larimer, "After a Teen Attempted Suicide, This Colorado Teacher Set Out to Show Her Students They Are Special," *Washington Post*, June 1, 2016. www.washingtonpost.com.

themselves again. According to a study from the National Institute of Mental Health (NIMH), CBT reduces repeat suicide attempts among youth and adults by 50 percent.

One CBT strategy that may be used is the creation of a hope box, which may be an actual box or merely a figurative one. Individuals use the box to store actual objects or collect thoughts and ideas that have special meaning to them and that they consider important for the future. Many in CBT also work with their therapist to come up with their own safety plan, which includes a list of their coping strategies, reasons for living, triggers for suicidal thoughts, and names and phone numbers of emergency contacts.

Another counseling approach that is effective in helping suicidal teens is dialectical behavioral therapy (DBT). This is a form of

CBT that involves a combination of individual therapy, skills training, and phone coaching. Those undergoing DBT usually meet with an individual counselor once a week for an hour to an hour and a half. In addition, they attend a weekly skills group—classes that help people learn to regulate their emotions and tolerate stress. DBT clients also agree to call their individual counselor for help if they feel a desire to hurt themselves; the counselor will coach them over the phone on alternatives to self-harm or suicide.

One person who was helped by DBT is Kate Wren, who attempted suicide at age sixteen by overdosing on pills. She met weekly with a therapist who helped her learn to manage her depression and self-destructive thoughts. She also learned to recognize her own triggers for depression, which included feeling overwhelmed and being criticized by others, and to change her pattern of thinking. In addition, Wren learned to focus on her well-being by doing things she finds enjoyable and relaxing, such as reading, making jewelry, knitting, and horseback riding. She created a "wellness box" for herself that contains a CD of soothing music, a jar of scented hand cream, and a pair of knitting needles and a ball of yarn. Today, Wren credits DBT with changing her outlook on life. "I used to think, 'When are they going to fix me and give me a magic pill?' I realized I was the only person who can prevent myself from killing myself."[67]

> "I used to think, 'When are they going to fix me and give me a magic pill?' I realized I was the only person who can prevent myself from killing myself."[67]
>
> —Kate Wren, who attempted suicide at age sixteen

Group Therapy and Support Groups

Group therapy and support groups have also been shown to be effective with teens. One type of group therapy is family focused therapy, which can be helpful for a teen whose depression and suicidal thoughts stem from family issues. One example is Attachment Based Family Therapy, developed to help suicidal teens reconnect with their families by learning better communication and problem-solving skills. Studies have shown that this type of therapy is also effective in helping depressed and suicidal LGBTQ teens.

Support groups are another effective way for teens to deal with depression and suicidal thoughts. Typically, a support group is made up of people with similar concerns who meet regularly to discuss their issues and offer empathy and understanding to one another. Many support groups are led by a trained counselor, but others may be led by peers who have also survived a suicide attempt. "Support groups can be helpful because they allow you to meet others who have had experiences similar to yours," explains SAMHSA. "It can be a huge relief to learn that you're not alone and that there are others who feel the way you do. It also can be helpful to learn about strategies others have found useful."[68]

One advantage to group therapy and support groups is that the affinity participants in the groups feel for one another because of their shared experiences may allow them to open up in ways they would not feel comfortable doing with someone who has not gone through the same thing. Suicide survivor Jordan Burnham says of his support group: "There were things that I told complete strangers because I knew that they understood where I was coming from. And I couldn't say that to my therapist, I couldn't say that to my parents, I couldn't say that to my friends because they didn't truly understand."[69]

Inpatient Treatment Centers

Both individual and group therapy are offered in residential, or inpatient, treatment centers. Residential treatment centers provide inpatient acute care as well as follow-up programs and therapy. One example is Village Behavioral Health in Louisville, Tennessee, which offers residential treatment to adolescents for a variety of issues, including depression and suicidal thoughts and actions.

One drawback to residential treatment centers is that they can be very costly. In addition, there is a lack of research on whether staying in such centers or in the psychiatric unit of a hospital is effective in preventing suicide. However, as child psychiatrist Benjamin Shain points out:

> Although no controlled studies have been conducted to prove that admitting adolescents at high risk to a psychiatric unit saves lives, likely the safest course of action is hospitalization, thereby placing the adolescent in a safe and protected environment. An inpatient stay will allow time for a complete medical and psychiatric evaluation with initiation of therapy in a controlled setting as well as arrangement of appropriate mental health follow-up care.[70]

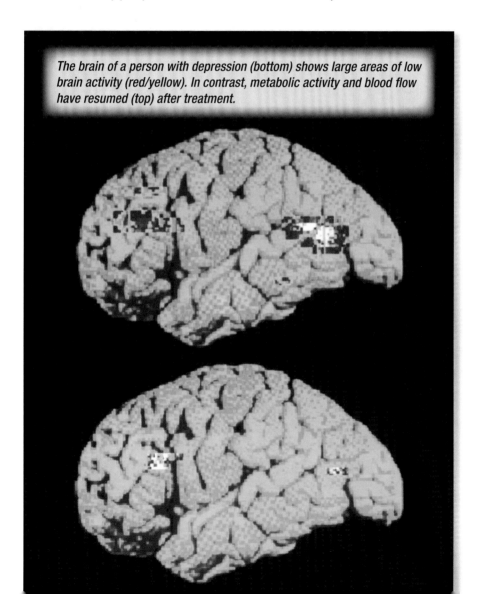

The brain of a person with depression (bottom) shows large areas of low brain activity (red/yellow). In contrast, metabolic activity and blood flow have resumed (top) after treatment.

Megan Rotatori, who attempted suicide at age seventeen by overdosing on prescription medication, is one example of a teen who sought help at a residential treatment center. Her experience was a positive one. She learned to deal with her depression by becoming more mindful of her feelings, being more accepting of things that she could not change, and relying on her friends and family for emotional support during difficult times. She explains her experience at the treatment center:

> My parents looked into a few things, and I decided I was going to go into a women's program at a hospital in Rhode Island. Basically, I wouldn't just be on lockdown so I wouldn't hurt myself, I would actually learn skills to try and deal with things. It was a DBT program only for women. I was the youngest girl in the program because I wasn't even 18 at the time and technically you were supposed to be over 18, but they made an exception so I could get into it, so I did that. I think I did that for a week. I got to come home that night and sleep in my own bed, which was really nice, and then I would be there all day learning skills: how to deal with things, talking to therapists, getting medications fixed, and stuff like that. That was literally the best thing that has happened to me.[71]

Antidepressants and Teens

Sometimes counseling alone is not enough to be effective in alleviating depression or suicidal thinking. In such cases, antidepressant medication may be prescribed by a qualified physician or psychiatrist. Antidepressants work by regulating the brain's neurotransmitters, which are out of balance in a depressed or suicidal person. These neurotransmitters affect mood and emotions, so medication can help improve the way a person feels. "Antidepressants can help jump-start mood and give people the boost they need to get over the symptoms of their depression," explains Eric Endlich, a clinical psychologist based in Boston. "This often allows them to start doing the things they enjoy again and make

Helping a Friend in Need

On the website of the Society for the Prevention of Teen Suicide, Christine Henderson, an advocate for youth suicide prevention, gives words of advice on what to do if a friend is thinking or talking about suicide:

Time is the crucial thing when dealing with a friend who is having suicidal thoughts. It is important that once you hear your friend talking about these feelings, to recognize them for what they are: a serious threat to your friend's life. Don't ignore them and assume the person is just being dramatic. If your friend is talking about killing him- or herself, you just can't handle it on your own—you HAVE TO tell a trusted adult! This may seem like something you hear all the time: tell an adult. But in this case, we're talking about someone's existence on earth, someone's life. That is something that should grab your attention and motivate you to tell someone immediately. Don't be a fool and think you can take care of this yourself—you can't! . . .

If you get the slightest inkling that someone might not be okay, do something about it! Don't wait around. And don't try to be a rescuer and take care of it on your own to save the friendship. Act on your instincts, trust your gut, be a grown-up, and tell! It could save the life of someone very dear to you.

Christine Henderson, "When a Friend Is Talking About Suicide," Society for the Prevention of Teen Suicide, 2016. www.sptsusa.org.

better choices for themselves, which also helps contribute to a more positive mood."[72]

Most experts agree that the use of antidepressants in teens (as in adults) works best when done in combination with counseling. This has been demonstrated in several studies. One such study undertaken by the NIMH in 2004 compared the use of the antidepressant fluoxetine (brand names Prozac and Sarafem) and CBT, alone and in combination, for treating depression in 439 adolescents aged twelve to seventeen. The researchers found that more than 60 percent of the kids who received only the antidepressant improved—but nearly 75 percent who received the combined treatment experienced an improvement. Additionally, the researchers found that the combination treatment was nearly twice as effective in improving symptoms of depression in teens than with CBT alone.

However, not all antidepressants work in teens. In a 2016 study published in the *Lancet*, researchers looked at the effects of fourteen different antidepressants in more than five thousand children and teens with major depressive disorder. The study found that of the fourteen antidepressants, only fluoxetine was more effective in alleviating symptoms of depression in youth than a placebo (a pill with no medical effects).

Other Drawbacks to Antidepressants

One potential drawback to treating suicidal people with antidepressants is that the medications can take up to eight weeks to start having an effect. Many people think the medication will immediately stop the suicidal thoughts, but antidepressants take time to work. Says Lisa Brennan, who takes medication to combat depression, "You definitely have to be a little patient for the medicine to work. For me, the change was very subtle at first, and then I realized that I really was feeling better. But it takes a few weeks."[73]

Additionally, the same medication may not work the same way for everyone, so different people need different antidepressants. Sometimes there is a trial-and-error period where the doctor—usually a psychiatrist, but sometimes a regular physician—may try a different medication. Brennan comments,

I had to try a couple of different kinds of medications to find the right one for me. One medication worked for a little while, and then I started to feel depressed again. So my doctor switched me to another medication, and that one is working great. It's just a matter of sticking with it and letting your doctor know how you're feeling.[74]

All medications have side effects, and antidepressants are no exception. These can include fatigue, drowsiness, nausea, constipation, and dry mouth, among others. Most of these side effects lessen or disappear with time. Anyone taking antidepressants, teens as well as adults, must weigh the inconvenience of their side effects against the benefit they receive from taking their medication. For some people the lift in their mood and thinking is worth any unpleasant side effects they may experience. Others may feel that the side effects are too much of a trade-off and decide to stop taking their medication.

When a person stops taking antidepressants, this can lead to another problem: There can be a withdrawal reaction to stopping the medication. This means that when individuals stop taking a particular medicine, they may soon experience a number of

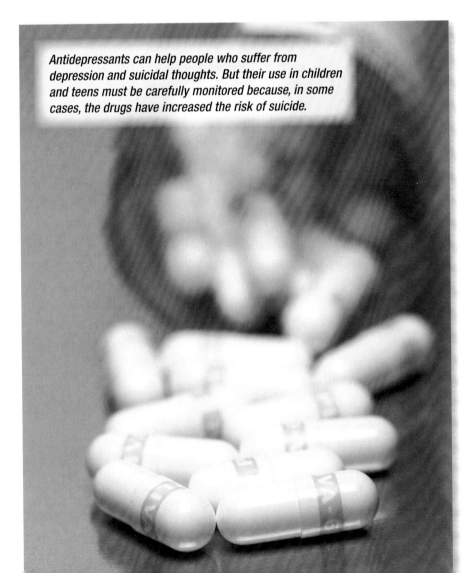

Antidepressants can help people who suffer from depression and suicidal thoughts. But their use in children and teens must be carefully monitored because, in some cases, the drugs have increased the risk of suicide.

symptoms such as anxiety, insomnia, and vivid dreams. "People have difficulty when they stop the medicine abruptly," says Richard Kadison, director of student health services at Harvard University. This is a concern because "adolescents are, in general, not the most reliable folks when it comes to taking medications."[75]

Some stop taking their antidepressants because of side effects, but there are other reasons a person may decide to stop. Some people do not like the idea of using chemicals to regulate their emotions, as psychologist Stephen A. Diamond explains: "Many patients reflexively resist taking psychiatric medication because they believe they *should* be able to manage their lives without it."[76] Others may stop taking their medication for different reasons. Melanie Demoree, who survived a suicide attempt at age seventeen, says, "I thought it was going to be an easy fix but it, of course, is not. Finding the right thing that works for you; that was hard. Then I stopped taking it for a while because I was not comfortable with being on it and I didn't want to be on it for my whole life 'cause I just—'cause of the stigma."[77]

Whatever their reason to stop taking their medication, people should always consult with their doctor first, because stopping antidepressants can have dangerous consequences. People who do so suddenly or without supervision can spiral back into depression and suicidal thinking. Sixteen-year-old Ian Hartley of Charlotte, Michigan, had been taking antidepressants for his depression, but he stopped taking them after only a couple of months. Although his parents were able to get him to start his medication again, experts say that antidepressants—like any medication—are less effective when taken irregularly. Hartley's depression worsened over the next three weeks, until one afternoon in May 2016 when he jumped from a bridge over Interstate 69 to the highway below. He died from his injuries shortly after he was taken to the hospital.

Black Box Warning

There are other potential dangers associated with the use of antidepressants in children and teens. Researchers have found that some antidepressants can actually worsen symptoms of depression in youths. Therefore, in 2004 the US Food and Drug Administration (FDA) issued a black box warning stating that antidepressants can actually increase the risk of suicidal thoughts and actions in children, teens, and young adults. A black box warning is the strictest warning applied to prescription drugs in the United States. As a result of this warning, many doctors have become reluctant to prescribe antidepressants to youths.

In the years since the black box warning was issued, however, subsequent research has indicated that the antidepressants only rarely increase the risk of suicidal thinking and behavior in youths. Many therefore believe that the benefits of antidepressants outweigh the risks, although their use in children and adolescents must be closely monitored by the prescribing physician.

> "Experiencing depression is part of the human experience but is not who you are as a whole. Do not let this take over your entire identity."[80]
>
> —Amanda Redhead, a registered nurse who attempted suicide as a teen

Despite the various problems and issues associated with antidepressant medication, experts maintain they are an effective way to treat depression and suicidal thoughts in teens. However, as psychologist Stephen A. Diamond stresses, the appropriate way to use them is in conjunction with counseling:

> Antidepressants are not a panacea. Sometimes, as with all medicines, there are unwelcome side-effects. Drugs can't change the patient's stressful circumstances. Nor can neurochemistry exorcise his or her inner demons. Which is why depressed patients also need supportive psychotherapy to help them move forward in life, despite their discouragement, self-doubts, insecurities and fears. . . .
>
> Yes, taking medication at some point may be a crucial part of the patient's responsibility for getting better; but it is no substitute for real psychotherapy.[78]

A Complex Issue

Teen suicide is a complex issue. There are many ways to approach prevention, intervention, and treatment. But the reality, as Benjamin Shain notes, is this: "Suicide risk can only be reduced, not eliminated, and risk factors provide no more than guidance."[79]

The words and experiences of those who have contemplated or attempted suicide offer perhaps the best guidance of all. In an open letter to youth published in the *Huffington Post*, Amanda Redhead offers words of hope to teens who are contemplating suicide:

> You are not your depression. This is not you. This experience will forever change you and be a part of you, but it is not and will never be the real you. This is not the way you are going to feel for your entire life. This is a temporary chemical disruption of your brain, nothing more. Experiencing depression is part of the human experience but is not who you are as a whole. Do not let this take over your entire identity.[80]

SOURCE NOTES

Introduction: A Vulnerable Population

1. Quoted in Alexandra Zaslow, "After Suicide of Teen David Molak, Texas Family Petitions Against Cyberbullying," *Today*, January 13, 2016. www.today.com.
2. Quoted in Madalyn Mendoza, "Alamo Heights Student Was a Victim of Bullying Before Committing Suicide, Family Says," *San Antonio (TX) Express-News*, January 8, 2016. www.my sanantonio.com.
3. Quoted in Paul Farrell, "David Molak: 5 Fast Facts You Need to Know," Heavy, January 13, 2016. http://heavy.com.
4. Lucie Hemmen, "Teens and Suicide," *Psychology Today*, June 17, 2013. www.psychologytoday.com.
5. Mayo Clinic, "Tween and Teen Health," 2016. www.mayo clinic.org.
6. Mark Gregston, "Suicide Epidemic Among Teens," Heartlight Ministries, 2016. www.heartlightministries.org.

Chapter One: The Problem of Teen Suicide

7. American Academy of Child & Adolescent Psychiatry, "Teen Suicide," 2013. www.aacap.org.
8. Quoted in Rebecca Ruiz, "Suicides Spike for 10 to 14-Year-Olds," Mashable, April 23, 2016. http://mashable.com.
9. Quoted in Steve Sadin, "Teen Suicide Rate Climbs," *Daily North Shore* (Highwood, IL), June 27, 2016. http://jwcdaily.com.
10. Youth Suicide Prevention Program, "After an Attempt," 2011. http://yspp.org.
11. Centers for Disease Control and Prevention, "Understanding Suicide," fact sheet, 2015. www.cdc.gov.
12. Quoted in Rae Ellen Bichell, "Suicide Rates Climb in U.S., Especially Among Adolescent Girls," *Morning Edition*, National Public Radio, April 22, 2016. www.npr.org.

13. Quoted in Bichell, "Suicide Rates Climb in U.S., Especially Among Adolescent Girls."

14. Quoted in Eilene Summer, "Teen Angst Turns Deadly," *Psychology Today*, January 1, 2009. www.psychologytoday.com.

15. Quoted in Bichell, "Suicide Rates Climb in U.S., Especially Among Adolescent Girls."

16. Jason Foundation, "Youth Suicide Statistics," 2016. http://jasonfoundation.com.

17. Quoted in National Institute of Mental Health, "Cognitive Therapy Reduces Repeat Suicide Attempts by 50 Percent," press release, August 2, 2005. www.nimh.nih.gov.

18. American Academy of Pediatrics Committee on Adolescence, "Suicide and Suicide Attempts in Adolescents," *Pediatrics*, April 2000. http://pediatrics.aappublications.org.

19. Quoted in Maggie Fox, "CDC Finds Troubling Rise in Teen Suicide Method," NBC News, March 5, 2015. www.nbcnews.com.

Chapter Two: Why Do Teens Commit Suicide?

20. Quoted in Sophie Saint Thomas, "What Is Life Like After Attempting Suicide?," Vice, September 13, 2015. www.vice.com.

21. Youth Suicide Prevention Program, "Youth Suicide Frequently Asked Questions (FAQ)," 2011. http://yspp.org.

22. Substance Abuse and Mental Health Services Administration, *A Journey Toward Health & Hope*. Rockville, MD: Substance Abuse and Mental Health Services Administration, 2015, p. 1.

23. Youth Suicide Prevention Program, "Youth Suicide Frequently Asked Questions (FAQ)."

24. Melanie Demoree, "I Survived a Suicide Attempt: Melanie Demoree," *Live Through This* (blog), April 7, 2014. http://livethroughthis.org.

25. Demoree, "I Survived a Suicide Attempt: Melanie Demoree."

26. Society for the Prevention of Teen Suicide, "Teens," 2016. www.sptsusa.org.

27. Quoted in Cristina Corbin, "Grim Headlines, Hard Data Show Suicides on Rise Among Teens Nationally," Fox News, February 4, 2016. www.foxnews.com.

28. William Coryell, "Can We Reduce Youth Suicides by Understanding and Identifying Risk Factors?," Care for Your Mind, April 22, 2014. http://careforyourmind.org.

29. Quoted in Paul Schankman, "Warrenton Parents Say Bullying Caused Daughter to Take Her Life," Fox 2 Now, April 26, 2016. http://fox2now.com.

30. Quoted in American Academy of Pediatrics, "With Suicide Now Teens' Second-Leading Cause of Death, Pediatricians Urged to Ask About Its Risks," June 27, 2016. www.aap.org.

31. Quoted in Mary MacVean, "After a Suicide, Classmates Often Think About It, Too, Study Says," Los Angeles Times, May 20, 2013. http://articles.latimes.com.

32. Quoted in Brandy Zadrozny, "Teen Copycat Suicides Are a Real Phenomenon," Daily Beast, May 1, 2014. www.thedailybeast.com.

33. Cathryn Rodway et al., "Suicide in Children and Young People in England: A Consecutive Case Series," Lancet, May 25, 2016. www.thelancet.com.

34. Quoted in JoNel Aleccia, "Teens More Stressed-Out than Adults, Survey Shows," NBC News, February 11, 2014. www.nbcnews.com.

35. Quoted in Hanna Rosin, "The Silicon Valley Suicides," Atlantic, December 2015. www.theatlantic.com.

36. Taylor Chiu, "Taylor Parker Chiu—Out of the Darkness," Momentum for Mental Health, September 20, 2015. www.momentumformentalhealth.org.

37. Quoted in Rosin, "The Silicon Valley Suicides."

Chapter Three: What Is It like to Live with Suicidal Feelings?

38. Rebecca Perkins, "Trying to Find the Light at the End of the Depression Tunnel," The Blog, Huffington Post, May 17, 2015. www.huffingtonpost.com.

39. Amanda Redhead, "An Open Letter to Young People Struggling, from a Suicide Survivor," *The Blog*, *Huffington Post*, January 26, 2016. www.huffingtonpost.com.

40. Quoted in CBN, "Kristen Anderson: Suicide Interrupted," 2016. www1.cbn.com.

41. Chiu, "Taylor Parker Chiu—Out of the Darkness."

42. Carl E. Pickhardt, "Adolescent Apathy and What Loss of Caring Can Mean," *Psychology Today*, May 28, 2012. www.psychologytoday.com.

43. Karen A., "Held Down by Depression," *L.A. Youth*, September 2011. www.layouth.com.

44. American Academy of Child & Adolescent Psychiatry, "Depression in Children and Teens," 2013. www.aacap.org.

45. Quoted in Rachel Greco, "Family of Teen Who Committed Suicide Fighting for Change," *Lansing (MI) State Journal*, May 19, 2016. www.lansingstatejournal.com.

46. Joe Taraszka, "My Struggle with Depression," *L.A. Youth*, May–June 2003. www.layouth.com.

47. Mike Woodard, "Our Daughter's Attempted Suicide," Thoughts About God, 2016. www.thoughts-about-god.com.

48. Megan Rotatori, "I Survived a Suicide Attempt: Megan Rotatori," *Live Through This* (blog), April 5, 2014. http://livethroughthis.org.

49. Kristen Anderson, "In Her Own Words," Reaching You Ministries. www.reachingyouministries.com.

50. Quoted in CBN, "Kristen Anderson: Suicide Interrupted."

51. Quoted in Corey Adwar, "The Role of Impulsiveness Is One of the Saddest Things About Suicide," Business Insider, August 13, 2014. www.businessinsider.com.

52. Arthur Curtis, e-mail message to author, August 8, 2016.

53. Quoted in WBTW News 13, "Family Works to Shed Light on Depression After Losing 17-Year-Old to Suicide," May 5, 2016. http://wbtw.com.

54. Quoted in Substance Abuse and Mental Health Services Administration, *A Journey Toward Health & Hope*, p. 1.

55. Quoted in Substance Abuse and Mental Health Services Administration, *A Journey Toward Health & Hope*, p. 8.

56. Rotatori, "I Survived a Suicide Attempt: Megan Rotatori."
57. Quoted in Leslie Scrivener, "People Who Attempted Suicide as Youths Trace Their Recovery," *Toronto Star*, December 3, 2011. www.thestar.com.
58. Redhead, "An Open Letter to Young People Struggling, from a Suicide Survivor."
59. Quoted in Substance Abuse and Mental Health Services Administration, *A Journey Toward Health & Hope*, p. 5.
60. Quoted in Sheryl Ubelacker, "Suicide Risk Remains High After First Attempt, Can Persist for Years," *Toronto Globe and Mail*, April 1, 2015. www.theglobeandmail.com.
61. Candace Paige, personal interview with author, August 15, 2016.
62. Kay Redfield Jamison, "Suicide in the Young: An Essay," Dana Foundation, July 1, 2001. http://dana.org.

Chapter Four: How Can Teen Suicide Be Prevented?

63. Jason Foundation, "Common Myths," 2016. http://jason foundation.com.
64. Cheryl King, "Strategies for Addressing Youth Suicide—and the Barriers to Effective Treatment," Care for Your Mind, May 14, 2014. http://careforyourmind.org.
65. Jason Foundation, "Signs & Concerns," 2016. http://jason foundation.com.
66. Hemmen, "Teens and Suicide."
67. Quoted in Scrivener, "People Who Attempted Suicide as Youths Trace Their Recovery."
68. Substance Abuse and Mental Health Services Administration, *A Journey Toward Health & Hope*, p. 20.
69. Quoted in Substance Abuse and Mental Health Services Administration, *A Journey Toward Health & Hope*, p. 20.
70. Benjamin Shain, "Suicide and Suicide Attempts in Adolescents," *Pediatrics*, June 2016. http://pediatrics.aappublica tions.org.
71. Rotatori, "I Survived a Suicide Attempt: Megan Rotatori."

72. Quoted in Ellen Greenlaw, "How Depression Medicine Can Affect Your Life," WebMD. www.webmd.com.

73. Quoted in Greenlaw, "How Depression Medicine Can Affect Your Life."

74. Quoted in Greenlaw, "How Depression Medicine Can Affect Your Life."

75. Quoted in Hara Estroff Marano, "Antidepressants: The Kid Question," *Psychology Today*, February 1, 2004. www.psychologytoday.com.

76. Stephen A. Diamond, "The Psychology of Psychopharmacology," *Psychology Today*, April 18, 2008. www.psychologytoday.com.

77. Melanie Demoree, "I Survived a Suicide Attempt: Melanie Demoree."

78. Diamond, "The Psychology of Psychopharmacology."

79. Benjamin Shain, "Suicide and Suicide Attempts in Adolescents."

80. Redhead, "An Open Letter to Young People Struggling, from a Suicide Survivor."

RECOGNIZING SIGNS OF TROUBLE

Verbal clues that a teen is depressed and may be suicidal include statements such as:
- "I wish I were dead."
- "Everyone would be better off without me."
- "No one would care if I died."
- "My boyfriend/girlfriend won't even miss me."
- "I'm going to kill myself."
- "I don't belong here."
- "I wonder what it's like to die?"
- "Maybe my parents would love me more if I was dead."
- "I feel like a burden to everyone."
- "I feel like I'm not good enough."

Behavioral clues that a teen is depressed and may be suicidal include actions such as:
- Talking, writing, or joking about death or suicide
- Talking about hurting him- or herself
- Having an obsession with guns or knives
- Expressing feelings of hopelessness, despair, guilt, or feeling trapped
- Making comments about life having no meaning or purpose
- Withdrawing from friends and family
- Abusing alcohol or drugs
- Behaving recklessly, such as running into traffic or jumping from high places
- Giving away prized possessions
- Losing interest in favorite activities
- Hinting that he or she might not be around anymore
- Having trouble concentrating, thinking clearly, or making decisions
- Sleeping or eating much more or much less than usual
- Acting sad, irritable, anxious, or apathetic
- Believing things will never get better or never change
- Speaking in a monotone or giving monosyllabic answers
- Looking sad or crying easily

The following organizations offer help for teens and others suffering from suicidal feelings, as well as detailed information about depression and suicide.

American Academy of Child & Adolescent Psychiatry (AACAP)

3615 Wisconsin Ave. NW
Washington, DC 20016-3007
website: www.aacap.org

The AACAP conducts research on the evaluation, diagnosis, and treatment of psychiatric disorders in teens and children. Its website contains a section titled Teen Suicide that includes information for teens on coping with depression and finding help for themselves or their friends, as well as videos, a crisis hotline, and resources for families.

American Association of Suicidology (AAS)

5221 Wisconsin Ave. NW
Washington, DC 20015
website: www.suicidology.org

The AAS is a nonprofit group that focuses on suicide prevention, research, education, and support. Its website provides statistics, information on suicide warning signs, infographics, and information for crisis centers throughout the United States and Canada. The National Center for the Prevention of Youth Suicide, a division of the AAS, is accessible through the AAS website.

American Foundation for Suicide Prevention

120 Wall St., 29th Floor
New York, NY 10005
website: https://afsp.org

The nonprofit organization American Foundation for Suicide Prevention aims to raise awareness, fund scientific research, and provide resources and help to anyone affected by suicide. The foundation's website contains a blog called *Lifesaver News*, which discusses topics related to suicide and its prevention.

Crisis Text Line

website: www.crisistextline.org
Crisis Text Line provides free crisis intervention twenty-four hours a day via text message. Individuals can get help from a trained crisis counselor by texting "START" to 741-741.

Jason Foundation

18 Volunteer Dr.
Hendersonville, TN 37075
website: http://jasonfoundation.com

The Jason Foundation was founded by Clark Flatt after his sixteen-year-old son, Jason, committed suicide in 1997. The foundation's website contains a newsletter, facts and statistics, a list of risk factors and warning signs, and links to other organizations that can help.

National Suicide Prevention Lifeline

website: www.suicidepreventionlifeline.org

The National Suicide Prevention Lifeline at 1-800-273-8255 is available nationwide, twenty-four hours a day, to connect callers with a trained counselor at a crisis center in their area. The lifeline for Spanish speakers is at 1-888-628-9454. The website also has a "Click to Chat" button for those seeking help who prefer not to talk on the telephone.

Society for the Prevention of Teen Suicide

110 W. Main St.
Freehold, NJ 07728
website: www.sptsusa.org

Founded by two friends who lost teenage kids to suicide, the non-profit Society for the Prevention of Teen Suicide works to reduce the number of youth suicides and attempted suicides by fostering public awareness through educational training programs. Its website offers videos, a blog, and numerous resources for teens.

Suicide Awareness Voices of Education (SAVE)

8120 Penn Ave. South, Suite 470
Bloomington, MN 55431
www.save.org

SAVE works to prevent suicide through public awareness and education and serves as a resource for those touched by suicide. Its website offers a newsletter, brochures, events, articles, and links for various topics related to depression and suicide.

TeenHelp.com

website: www.teenhelp.com

TeenHelp.com works to educate teens and parents of teens on a variety of issues teens face, including depression and suicide. The TeenHelp.com website contains articles on teen mental health, teen sexual abuse and trauma, teen relationship issues, and many other topics.

Teen Suicide

website: www.teensuicide.us

The Teen Suicide website contains articles, statistics, and information on teen suicide, including warning signs and prevention options. The site includes links to outside organizations dedicated to teen suicide prevention.

Text-A-Tip

website: www.leadingefforts.org/text-a-tip

The Text-A-Tip system provides youth an anonymous way to get immediate help for themselves or others twenty-four hours a day by texting a message to 274-637 that begins with "847Help." Texts are answered by certified mental health professionals.

Trans Lifeline

2443 Fillmore St. #380-9468
San Francisco, CA 94115
website: www.translifeline.org

Trans Lifeline, a nonprofit organization dedicated to the well-being of transgender people of all ages, offers a hotline staffed by trained operators. In the United States, call 1-877-565-8860; in Canada, call 1-877-330-6366.

Trevor Project

PO Box 69232
West Hollywood, CA 90069
website: www.thetrevorproject.org

The Trevor Project focuses on crisis and suicide prevention among lesbian, gay, bisexual, transgender, and questioning youth. Its website offers information on suicide prevention, a blog, news, and a support center available via telephone call, online chat, or text message.

Books

Eric Hastings, *Teen Suicide: The Step-by-Step Guide to Coping and Dealing with Suicide*. Seattle, WA: Inphinity, 2014. Kindle edition.

Hal Marcovitz, *Teens & Suicide*. Broomall, PA: Mason Crest, 2014. Kindle edition.

Eric Marcus, *Why Suicide? Questions and Answers About Suicide, Suicide Prevention, and Coping with the Suicide of Someone You Know*. New York: HarperOne, 2013. Kindle edition.

Substance Abuse and Mental Health Services Administration, *A Journey Toward Health & Hope*. Rockville, MD: Substance Abuse and Mental Health Services Administration, 2015.

Christine Watkins, *Teen Suicide*. Farmington Hills, MI: Greenhaven, 2014.

Internet Sources

HealthyPlace, "Suicide Information, Resources & Support," August 12, 2015. www.healthyplace.com/other-info/suicide/suicide-suicidal-thoughts-and-behaviors-toc.

Kimberly Leonard, "Suicide Rate Triples Among Girls," *U.S. News & World Report*, April 22, 2016. www.usnews.com/news/articles/2016-04-22/cdc-suicide-deaths-on-the-rise-among-teen-girls-and-middle-aged-men.

Raychelle Cassada Lohmann, "The 'Why' Behind Teen Suicide," *Teen Angst* (blog), *Psychology Today*, June 18, 2014. www.psychologytoday.com/blog/teen-angst/201406/the-why-behind-teen-suicide.

National Institute of Mental Health, "Suicide Prevention," 2015. www.nimh.nih.gov/health/topics/suicide-prevention/index.shtml.

Kim Norvell, "Teen Survives Suicide Attempts to Reach Gradua-tion," *Des Moines (IA) Register*, May 25, 2016. www.desmoines register.com/story/news/local/west-des-moines/2016/05/25/iowa -teen-survives-suicide-attempts-reach-graduation/84506200.

Rose Palazzolo, "Preventing Teen Suicide," *Psychology Today*, June 9, 2016. www.psychologytoday.com/articles/200305/pre venting-teen-suicide.

WebMD, "Teen Depression," 2016. www.webmd.com/depression /guide/teen-depression.

INDEX

Note: Boldface page numbers indicate illustrations.

causes. *See* risk factor(s)
Centers for Disease Control
and Prevention (CDC)
on gender differences, 17–18
on number of attempted
versus completed suicides
annually, 10
on number of emergency
room admissions for self-
inflicted wounds, 8
on prevalence of suicide as
cause of teen deaths, 12,
15
on teen rate compared to
adult rate, 9–10
2015 survey of serious
consideration, plans, or
attempts, 11–12
See also National Center for
Health Statistics (NCHS)
Chiu, Taylor, 31–32, 35–36
clinical depression. *See*
depression
clusters of suicides, 29–30
cognitive behavioral therapy
(CBT), 48–49, 50, 55–56
copycat suicides, 29–30
Corcoran, Brittany, 40–41
Coryell, William, 26
counseling, 48–51, 55–56, 59
crisis intervention, 48
Curtin, Sally C., 10, 12
Curtis, Arthur, 38
cyberbullying, 4–5, 28–29

Darras, Brittni, 50
deaths
frequency of, 9
leading cause of teen, 12,
14–15
number of (2014), 9, **11**

teen, compared to adult
deaths, 9–10
use of firearms and, 18,
19–20
Demoree, Melanie, 23–24, 58
depression
and access to mental health
care, 16
apathy and, 36
brain and, 23–26, **53**
bullying and, 25
gender and, 17–18
and importance of expressing
feelings, 12
living with, 45
managing, 42
as risk factor, 22
signs of, 23, 38–39
stigma of, 41–42, 44
symptoms of, 22, 34–36
dialectical behavioral therapy
(DBT), 50–51
Diamond, Stephen A., 58, 59
drug abuse, 26

emergency room admissions,
and self-inflicted wounds, 8
Endlich, Eric, 54–55
ethnicity and suicide rate, 17

family therapy, 51–52
feelings
expressing, 12, 40–41
of guilt and shame, 42
importance of supporting,
47
Finkelstein, Yaron, 44–45
firearms
access to, 17, 19–20
gender and use of, 18
success using, 18–19

PICTURE CREDITS

Cover: Depositphotos/michaeldb

6: Depositphotos/photographee.eu

11: Maury Aaseng

14: Depositphotos/HighwayStarz

19: Depositphotos/monkeybusiness

23: Thinkstock Images/KatarzynaBialasiewicz

28: Thinkstock Images/iStockphoto/DGLimages

37: iStockphoto/strickke

43: Maury Aaseng

49: Shutterstock.com/Monkey Business Images

53: WDCN/University College of London/Science Source

57: GIPhotoStock/Science Source

ABOUT THE AUTHOR

Cherese Cartlidge holds a bachelor's degree in psychology and a master's degree in education. She is a freelance editor and the author of more than twenty books for children and young adults.